Romance Struggles?

Don Barnes

Published by Don Barnes, 2024.

This publication provides the Author's opinion and neither the publisher nor the author intends to render legal, accounting, or other professional advice with this publication.
The publisher and the author disclaim any personal liability, loss or risk incurred as a consequence of the use and application, directly or indirectly, of advice, information or methods presented in this publication.
First Edition

Copyright © 2025

By Don Barnes / Tryune Works!

TRYUNE WORKS! and Life works in threes are trademarks and copyrights of Don Barnes and Tryune Works!

 **LifeWorksInThrees.com**

Table of Contents

About the Author

Don is the founder and author of Life Works in Threes!™ E-books. He is a lifelong Texan who has traveled extensively while taking a keen interest in human behavior. His curiosity about life and what drives humans led him to the discovery of how life works in threes. He coined this term as the *Tryune Concept.*

Don attended college on an athletic scholarship and then embarked on a 30-year career in the oil and gas industry. Since the year 2000, he has been a consultant for distributors and manufacturers of various industries. Along the way, he worked on his Tryune discovery in hopes of someday sharing his findings with those struggling unnecessarily... in life. What Don surmised from 40+ years of R&D was that people were struggling unnecessarily because they were not aware that "life works in threes." They, for the most part, have been living their lives <u>by chance</u> rather than<u> by choice,</u> he also discovered.

From this, he began focusing on the "mechanics of life" which shows formulas for success with subjects such as *life, health, money, purpose and so forth.* When people are able to grasp the Tryune Concept, they can apply the formulas with topics that interest them and begin eliminating the struggle. This epiphany is what triggered his Tryune venture and is now on the path of sharing with all who desire to improve on their lives.

Don currently resides in Southern California and Texas while overseeing his businesses and investments.

Life Works in Threes™

When I was a kid growing up, no one sat me down and said, "Okay Don, I'm going to show you how life works so that you can navigate your way through adulthood." I graduated from school, got married and went about my way with the "learn as you go" concept. It was kind of like putting together a backyard swing set without a set of instructions. Lots of frustration and do-overs, for sure!

My discovery of the "triune" word and noticing how things come together in threes is really what set me off on researching that maybe "life comes in three" ...sort of a mechanical approach to managing life, if you will. I combed the libraries and bookstores for information on this and found one book on the subject that was written back in 1951. The author's name was John S. Arant.

What Mr. Arant had to say is this "For lack of a better name, I have called this *The Triangle of Triumph* and therefore, consistent with the name, since most of these conclusions are built on the geometric figure of the triangle." He continued "All Life and all lives are seated in, and circumscribed by, the triangle. The Author and Source and Director of all life is Himself triune in character – Father, Son, and Holy Spirit. Man is of triple nature – body, mind, and spirit – and within those three there are many triangles – desires, development, decay; intellect, will, sensibilities. Of this "paced interlude in the midst of eternity" which we call time there is the triangle of Past, Present, and Future. Space – that limitless and measureless element of the physical universe – is best known in terms of Height, Breadth, and Depth. Try building yourself some triangles along the lines of your Will, your Work, your Way – You will find some interesting angles.

So, for the first time, I realized that life is designed in a mechanical way to come in threes. That means you don't have to rely on wishing and hoping things turn out okay. You can actually look at the three parts that a particular thing is made of and then apply them to get what you're wanting. Like a three-ingredient recipe or a combination lock. With a combination lock, you need the three exact numbers to unlock the lock…otherwise you will continue to struggle.

Some 40 years later, I accumulated things that work in threes and that's when I knew I needed to share this with anyone wanting answers. To have success/harmony in your life, just apply the three parts of an area you're working on, and things will fall into place. I also learned that the recipe for success with just about anything is by doing these three things, consistently – THINK positively, SPEAK positively and ACT positively. For example, if I want to be a successful artist. I would think to myself "I can do this because I have the talent." Then I would speak it this way "Yes, I am working on my art degree and plan to do portraits professionally." Finally, I would act on that by taking art classes and continue crafting my skill. Eventually, I will see the positive results/success I'm looking for.

Conversely, if I think positively but speak negatively…it will cancel out. Or if I speak positively but have no positive action going on…nothing will happen.

I looked up "How Life Works" and "The Mechanics of Life" and these are really talking about the biology of how our cells work and other chemistry. TRYUNE WORKS! teaches that life is kind of like building blocks. Pick a topic you may be struggling with. See the three parts that topic consists of and then start applying them…on a consistent basis. That will help you overcome the struggle and get you back in harmony/success with how life works.

For 30+ years I was a golf instructor (by accident). My two kids had some success playing junior golf and so friends and neighbors would ask me to show them and their kids how to play golf successfully. From all of this, I got pretty good at watching golfers on the driving range and could spot right away why they were struggling with hitting bad golf shots. I was able to do that because I knew the three steps to hitting good golf shots. I learned them from studying golf and played for several decades. I "broke the code" for me so to speak.

So now you know that life works in threes. You can live your life *by choice* rather than *by chance* and that my friend... is the key to a fulfilling life.

LIFE WORKS
IN THREES!

My sanctuary on the Pacific coast

Introduction

Picture this: a relationship without romance is like a cake without frosting – it's missing that sweet, indulgent touch that makes it truly delightful. When there's a lack of romance, the once vibrant connection between partners can start to feel dull and uninspired. It's like going through the motions without the passion and excitement that make love feel alive.

One of the biggest ways that a lack of romance affects a relationship is by creating a sense of emotional distance between partners. Without those tender moments of affection and intimacy, it's easy for resentment and dissatisfaction to creep in. When gestures of love and appreciation become few and far between, partners may start to feel neglected or unimportant in each other's lives, leading to feelings of loneliness and disconnection.

Moreover, the absence of romance can also take a toll on the overall happiness and satisfaction within the relationship. Without those little sparks of excitement and joy, partners may begin to feel like they're missing out on the magic of being in love. It's like trying to enjoy a movie without popcorn – sure, you might still get through it, but it's just not as enjoyable or fulfilling. Ultimately, a lack of romance can leave partners feeling unfulfilled and questioning the strength of their bond, highlighting the importance of keeping the flame of romance alive in any relationship.

My discovery of the Tryune Concept

Before we dive into romance struggles and how to overcome them, let me share my discovery of the Tryune Concept and how life works in threes. It all began in the summer of 1982.

I grew up with parents who treated everyone with decency and respect. My three older sisters and I were raised in a home that was "middle-class traditional." We lived in modest homes in different small towns, attended school and church on a regular basis and celebrated all the traditional holidays. Eventually we settled during the spring of 1964 in the big city of Houston, Texas. I'll never forget the vastness of the city and hearing sirens from police cars, fire trucks and ambulances on a regular basis. I was excited and scared at the same time.

Once settled in this fast-paced city, I finished my growing-up years with an academic diploma and sweetheart intact. I got a job, bought a car, got married, bought a house and produced two beautiful babies in a span of about 5 years. Talk about having to grow up fast!

Things went from great in my childhood to absolute misery in my young adulthood. I began to struggle with my job because deep down I just hated what I was doing. This problem created a snowball effect because soon after, my weight, my finances, my relationships, my happiness and everything else worth saving was going down the drain. I eventually hit a level of frustration that I had never experienced before and didn't know how to get out of it. My cry for help was for anyone or anything to come to my rescue. I just ran out of solutions for my situation.

This is when my discovery happened.

One night shortly after my meltdown, while sleeping soundly, the word "triune" began to softly pound in my head like a mantra. I woke up a little startled and decided to go look up the word in my favorite dictionary (this was WAY before Google.) The definition said '**triune** (try-une) – 1) a group of three things; united. 2) Being 3 in 1 such as *humans are mental, physical and spiritual.* I scratched my head, got a glass of water and went back to bed.

The next day while driving around town, I began thinking about things that I was taught in my younger years that came in threes. My Boy Scout manual taught that to have **character**, I needed to be *1) physically strong,* 2) *mentally awake and 3) morally straight.* My high school football coach would say emphatically "If you want to be **a good football player**, you have to be *1) mobile 2) agile and 3) hostile*!" My first sales manager shared with me that to be **a successful salesman**, I needed to have *1) sales skills, 2) product knowledge and 3) a good image.*

"Hmm", I thought, "wonder if there are other examples out there of things that work in threes?" So, some 40 years later, I have researched and discovered that many, many things work in threes. What this message was telling me is that to achieve success or balance in any significant area of my life, the three things that area consisted of had to be present continuously. That's when I had my epiphany. This discovery was telling me the secret to how life <u>really</u> works.

Tryune is a play on the word "triune" as an invitation to "try" this concept. Furthermore, we do not say that life <u>only</u> works in threes. Life also works in ones, twos, fours and so on. What has been observed though is that the many things significant to life, just so happen to come and work in threes. That's what is being shared in this book.

Now, you are about to see 40+ years of research and proof that life works in threes. I did not make up any of these topics. I invite you to research them on the internet to validate what is written here. There are some interesting facts that most of us have never realized...until now.

How Life Works in Threes (around 200 examples)

LIFE

Humans consist of *body, mind and soul.*

A human's basic needs are *health, income and provisions.*

A human's basic wants are *comfort, gain and approval.*

Our minds are made up of the *conscious, the subconscious and the unconscious.*

Philosophy explains *the id, the ego and superego.*

Atoms consist of *protons, neutrons and electrons.*

Motion is explained by *three basic laws.*

Science falls under three main branches: *natural, social and formal sciences*

Time is *past, present and future*...at the same time.

Electricity consists of *ohms, amperes and voltage.*

Music's basic elements are *duration, pitch and timbre.*

Democracy is a government *of the people, by the people and for the people.*

U.S. branches of government are *the judicial, the executive and the legislative.*

Armed Forces protect us on *land, air and sea.*

Environmentally, we are asked *to reduce, recycle and re-use.*

The news program gives us *the news, sports and conditions.*

Our days consist of *morning, afternoon and evening.*

Three months in each season of the year

Our main meals are known as *breakfast, lunch and dinner.*

A balanced diet consists of *good proteins, carbohydrates and fats.*

Traditional Family consists of *father, mother, and child(ren)*

<u>SCIENCES</u>

Three major branches of natural science – *(physical, earth/ space and life sciences)*

Three major branches of modern physics - *(classical, relativistic, quantum)*

Three major branches of biology *(botany, zoology, microbiology)*

Three spatial dimensions: *height* (up/down), *width* (left/ right) and *depth* (forwards/backwards)

Three-gauge bosons (photon, gluon, W&Z bosons)

Three types of elementary particles *(leptons, quarks, gauge bosons)*

Three quarks in every proton *(two "up" and one "down")*

Three primary colors of light *(red, green, blue)*

Three color tone properties *(hue, value, chroma)*

Three laws of motion (*Newton's laws*)

Three laws of planetary motion (*Kepler's laws*)

Three layers of the Sun's interior (*core, radiative zone, convective zone*)

Three layers of the Sun's atmosphere (*photosphere, chromosphere, corona*)

Three types of meteorites (*iron, stony iron, stony*)

Three types of galaxy shapes (*elliptical, spiral, irregular*)

Three substances of the universe (*normal matter, 'dark matter', 'dark energy'*)

Three phases of the moon (*new moon, first quarter, full moon*)

Three planetary regions (*temperate, sub-tropical, tropical*)

Three layers of the Earth (*crust, mantle, core*)

Three components of an ecosystem (*producers, consumers, decomposers*)

Three types of rocks (*igneous, sedimentary, metamorphic*)

Three types of fossil fuels (*coal, crude oil, natural gas*)

Three hydrological processes (*evaporation, condensation, precipitation*)

Three basic types of (meteorological) precipitation (*liquid, freezing, frozen*)

Three types of substances *(mono-constituent, multi-constituent, UVCB)*

Three phases of (normal) matter *(solid, liquid, gas)*

Three types of covalent chemical bonds *(single, double and triple bonds)*

Three isotopes of hydrogen *(protium, deuterium, tritium)*

Three atoms in each molecule of water *(two hydrogen atoms and an oxygen atom)*

Three endings to salts *(-ide, -ite, -ate)*

Three requirements for fire *(fuel, oxygen, heat)*

Three nucleotide bases in a genetic codon

Three domains of life *(archaea, bacteria and eukaryotes)*

Three major groups of flowering plants *(monocots, eudicots, magnolids)*

Three major functions that are basic to plant growth and development: *(photosynthesis* [making sugars], *respiration* [metabolizing those sugars], and *transpiration* [water vapor loss]

Three things that the chlorophyll in plants needs for photosynthesis to take place: *(sunlight, carbon dioxide and water)*

Transpiration serves three roles: *(cooling the plant, moving minerals* and *sugars through the plant,* and *maintaining the turgidity pressure* [stiffness] *of the plant's cells)*

Three parts of an insect's body *(head, thorax, abdomen)*

BIOLOGY

Three types of cones in the retina, relating to the three primary colors

Three semi-circular canals in the ear *(lateral, anterior, posterior)*

Three sections in the ear *(outer, middle, inner)*

Three ossicles in the middle ear *(malleus, incus, stapes)*

Three segments to each limb *(proximal, mid, distal)*

Three bones in each arm *(humerus, radius, ulna)*

Three joints in the arm *(shoulder, elbow, wrist)*

Three joints in the leg *(hip, knee, ankle)*

Three joints in the elbow *(humeroulnar, humeroradial, proximal radioulnar)*

Three functional compartments in the knee joint *(the femoropatellar, medial femorotibial* and *lateral femorotibial articulations)*

Three types of fibrous joints *(sutures, gomphoses, syndesmoses)*

Three types of bone in each hand *(carpals, metacarpals, phalanges)*

Three types of bone in each foot *(tarsals, metatarsals, phalanges)*

Three bones (phalanges) in each finger and in each toe *(proximal, intermediate, distal)*

Three layers of skin *(dermis, epidermis, hypodermis)*

Three components of a cell *(cell membrane, nucleus, cytoplasm)*

Three types of blood vessels *(arteries, veins, capillaries)*

Three types of blood cells [*red* (erythrocytes), *white* (leukocytes), *platelets* (thrombocytes)]

Three processes of the intestinal tract *(ingestion, digestion, excretion)*

Three germ layers *(Endoderm, Mesoderm, Ectoderm)*

Three parts of a human tooth *(crown, neck, root)*

Three organs of otolaryngology *(ear, nose, throat)*

Three major body systems *(digestive, circulatory, respiratory)*

Three parts to a neuron: *(soma [cell body], axon, dendrites)*

Three main parts of the brain *(forebrain, midbrain, hindbrain)*

Three parts of the forebrain *(cerebrum, thalamus, hypothalamus)*

Three parts of the midbrain *(colliculi, tegmentum, cerebral peduncles)*

Three parts of the hindbrain *(cerebellum, pons, medulla)*

Three membranes enclosing the brain *(dura mater, arachnoid, pia mater)*

The brain operates on three levels: *consciously* (for cognitive thought and declarative memory); *subconsciously* (for pre-planned actions and procedural memory); and *unconsciously* (for breathing, heart beating, etc.)

Our conscious mind is fed from three sources: *our senses* (which can be fooled); *our memory* (which is flawed); and *our imagination* (which is inventive)

Three aspects of the human mind *(memory, intellect, will)*

Three parts of the human personality *(id, ego, superego)*

The sum of human capacity consists of three abilities *(thought, word and deed)*

Three times of man *(birth, life, death)*

Three periods of the Gait Cycle *(initial double limb support, single limb support, and terminal double limb support)*

MUSIC

Three types of musical notes *(sharps, flats, naturals)*

Three aspects of a song (*lyrics, melody, rhythm*)

Three types of musical chords (*root, third, fifth*)

MATHEMATICS

Three types of a real number (*positive, negative, zero*)

Three parts to any arithmetic operation: for addition: *augend, addend and sum* - for subtraction: *minuend, subtrahend and difference* - for multiplication: *multiplicand, multiplier and product* - for division: *dividend, divisor and quotient*

Three laws of arithmetic operations (*commutative, associative, distributive*)

Three types of equivalence relation (*reflexivity, symmetry, transitivity*)

Three types of symmetry operations (*translation, rotation, reflection*)

Three geometries (*Euclidean, spherical, hyperbolic*)

The number 3 is the basis of an entire branch of mathematics, called trigonometry (from the Greek *trigonon* "triangle" + *metron* "measure")

Three trigonometric functions (*sine, cosine, tangent*)

Three types of average (*mean, mode, median*)

GRAMMAR

Three logical operators (*AND, OR and NOT*)

Three laws of logic (*identity, noncontradiction, excluded middle*)

Three parts of a logical syllogism (*major premise, minor premise, conclusion*)

Three grammatical parts to a sentence (*subject, verb, complement*)

Three persons in grammar [*1st person* (I/we), *2nd* (you or your), *3rd* (he/she/it/they)]

Three genders in grammar [*masculine* (he/him), *feminine* (she/her), *neuter* (it)]

Three forms of comparison in grammar [*positive, comparative* (more, -er), *superlative* (most, -est)]

Three cases in (English) grammar [*subjective/nominative* (he), *objective/accusative* (him) and *possessive/genitive* (his)]

Three parts of a narrative (*beginning, middle, end*)

Components of an essay (*introduction, body, conclusion*)

Elements of a rhetorical appeal (*ethos, pathos, logos*)

Aspects of a story (*plot, characters, setting*)

<u>RELIGION</u>

The Creator – *omniscient, omnipotent, omnipresent*

Christian God – *Father, Son, Holy Spirit*

Jesus – *The Way, The Truth, The Life*

Ancient Near East- *Qudshu, Astarte, Anat*

Classical Antiquity – Many dieties came in threes

Hinduism – Para Brahman is *Brahma, Visnu, Shiva*

Ancient Celtic Cultures – *many example of triad dieties*

Buddhism – *The three jewels*

Taoism – *The three pure ones*

Islam – *Fear, Hope and Love*

Baha'i - *Intention, Power and Action*

Confucianism – *Benevolence, Wisdom and Courage*

<u>OTHER TRIUNE EXAMPLES</u>

3 Coins in a Fountain

3 Days of the Condor

3 Miles in a League

3 Goals in a Hat Trick

3 Piece Suit

3 Feet in a Yard

3 Books in Lord of the Rings

3 Ring Circus

3 Ships of Christopher Columbus

3 Sheets to the Wind

3 Books in a Trilogy

3 Wheels on a Tricycle

3 Wise Men

3-Legged Race

3 Ring Circus

3-Wheeler

3 Cornered Hat

3 Dimensional

3 Musketeers

3 R's (reading, 'riting, 'rithmatic)

3 Sides of a triangle

3 Races in the Triple Crown (horse racing)

3 Angles in a Triangle

3 Trimesters in a Pregnancy

3 Flavors in Neapolitan Ice Cream

3 Stars in Orion's belt

3 Barleycorns in an Inch

3 Hands on a Clock (with the Seconds Hand)

3 Colors in a Flag

3 Minute Egg

3 Great Pyramids at Giza

3 Holes in a Bowling Ball

3 Colors in a Set of Traffic Lights

3 Minutes in a Boxing Round

3 Teaspoons in a Tablespoon

3 Legs on a Stool

3 Monastic Vows (Obience, Stability, Conversatio Morum)

3 Body Types: Endomorph, Mesomorph, Ectomorph

3 Ring Notebooks

3 Germ layers: Endoderm, Mesoderm, Ectoderm

3 Species of Homo: Homo habilis, Homo erectus, Homo sapiens

3 Basic parts of a camera: Lens, Shutter, Sensor

3 Stages of a Project lifecycle: initiation, planning, execution

The Truth, The Whole Truth and Nothing but the Truth

Life, Liberty and the Pursuit of Happiness

Hear no Evil, See no Evil, Speak no Evil

National motto of France/Haiti: Liberty, Equality, Fraternity

Paper, Rock, Scissors

Ready, Aim, Fire

On Your mark, Get Set, Go

Olympic medals of gold, silver, bronze

Types of joints (ball & socket, hinge, pivot)

Stages of a rocket launch (launch, orbit, re-entry)

Parts of a joke (setup, delivery, punchline)

Primary components of a transistor (emitter, base, collector)

Primary components of an airplane (fuselage, wings, empennage)

Basic components of a computer: CPU, memory, storage

Three phases in the development of technology (*eotechnic* [*mechanical*], *paleotechnic* [*steam-powered*] and *neotechnic* [*electric-powered*]

Communication systems require three components (*transmitter, channel, receiver*)

The list goes on. See if you can find more examples as they are everywhere in our universe! Now that you know that life works in threes (with proof!), we can begin to apply this concept to whatever topics we want.

So, to overcome struggles in romance, we need to apply the three areas that romance consists of – APPETITE, COMMUNICATION and CREATIVE. Let's get started!

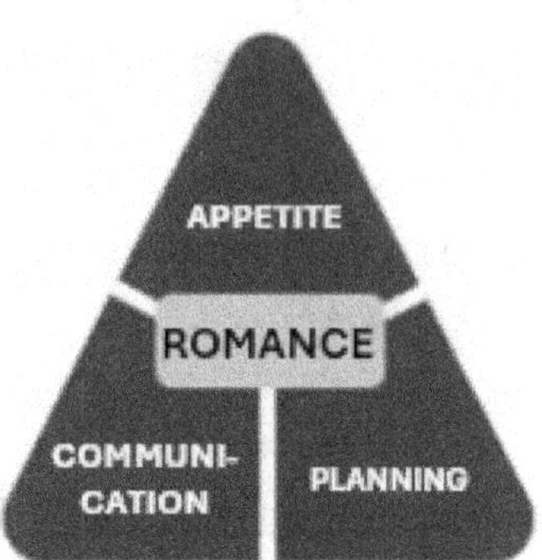
APPETITE
ROMANCE
COMMUNI-
CATION
PLANNING

ROMANCE

Romance in a relationship is like the sprinkle of magic dust that keeps the connection alive and thriving. It's not just about grand gestures or candlelit dinners (though those are lovely too), but it's the little moments of thoughtfulness and affection that build the foundation of intimacy and understanding between partners. Imagine a relationship without those sweet surprises, stolen kisses, or heartfelt gestures; it would be like a flower without sunlight – it might survive, but it won't truly flourish.

Romance adds excitement and spark to the routine of daily life. Whether it's leaving a love note on the fridge or planning a surprise weekend getaway, these gestures inject freshness into the relationship, reminding both partners of the love and passion they share. Moreover, romance fosters a deeper emotional connection by creating opportunities for vulnerability and openness. When partners take the time to express their love and admiration for each other, it strengthens their bond and reinforces their commitment to one another.

Beyond its emotional significance, romance also plays a practical role in maintaining a healthy relationship. It serves as a reminder of the importance of prioritizing each other amidst life's myriad distractions. In the midst of busy schedules and responsibilities, making time for romance demonstrates a commitment to nurturing the relationship and keeping the flame burning bright. So, whether it's a spontaneous picnic in the park or a cozy night in... watching old movies, never underestimate the power of romance in keeping your relationship vibrant and fulfilling.

 DON BARNES

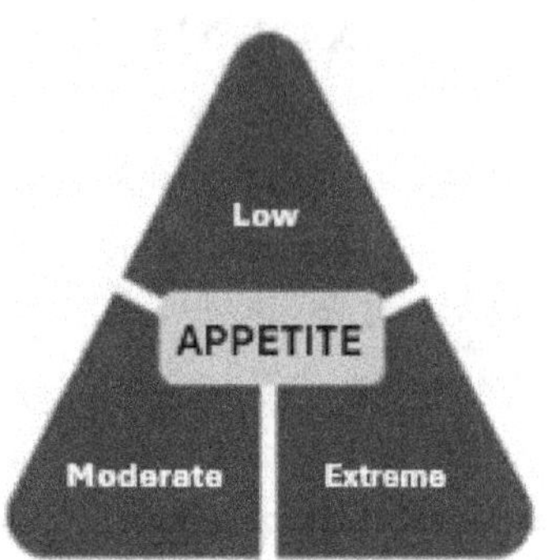

APPETITE

In every relationship, the dynamics of mutual romantic desire play a crucial role in shaping its depth and longevity. Picture it like a dance where partners move in sync, their steps perfectly aligned to the rhythm of their shared affection. However, just like any dance, it's essential that the levels of desire match up – whether it's low, moderate, or extreme – to maintain harmony and satisfaction.

When both partners have a **low level of romantic desire**, it's like two puzzle pieces that fit together seamlessly. While the intensity of their passion may not be off the charts, their contentment lies in the simplicity of their connection. They find joy in their everyday moments, cherishing the comfort and companionship they bring to each other's lives. Their relationship may not be filled with grand gestures, but it's grounded in a deep sense of understanding and mutual respect.

On the other hand, when partners have a **moderate level of romantic desire**, it's like a gentle breeze that breathes life into their relationship. They enjoy expressing their love through thoughtful gestures and spontaneous acts of affection, keeping the flame of romance burning bright. While their desire may not reach fever pitch levels, they find fulfillment in nurturing their connection and creating lasting memories together. Their relationship is a perfect balance of passion and practicality, where love grows stronger with each passing day.

Extreme desire is a whole 'nother level! If both partners have this appetite, then nearly every encounter is like the 4th of July! Conversely, if one partner has a low or moderate desire, it can be tricky making it work. Typically, romance issues have a lot to do with desire compatibility – he wants it more or less and she wants it more or less. Working this out is the key to keeping romance alive.

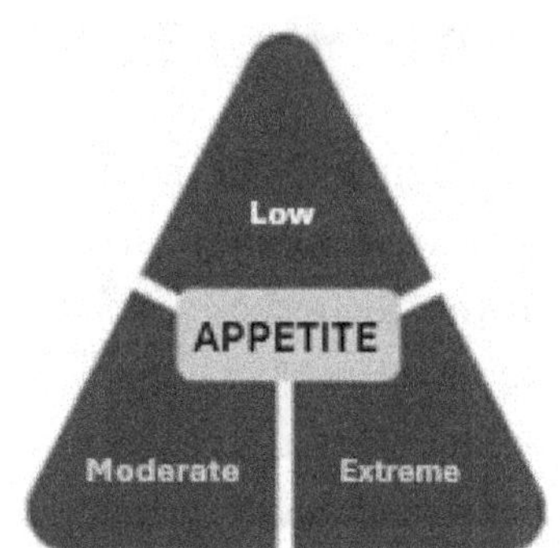
Low
APPETITE
Moderate
Extreme

Low

In a relationship where one or both partners have a low level of romantic desire, the dynamics may differ from those characterized by intense passion, but they're no less valuable or fulfilling. It's like enjoying a slow dance under the stars – gentle, comforting, and deeply intimate. While the flames of passion may not burn as brightly, the warmth of companionship and understanding envelops the relationship like a cozy blanket.

In such dynamics, **partners find solace in the simplicity of their connection.** They may not shower each other with grand gestures or profess their love in extravagant ways, but they cherish the quiet moments of togetherness. From sharing a meal to cuddling on the couch, their bond is grounded in a deep sense of familiarity and acceptance. Their love may not be flashy, but it's steady and unwavering, like a lighthouse guiding them through life's storms.

Despite the lower levels of romantic desire, these relationships thrive on mutual respect and appreciation. Partners understand each other's needs and preferences, creating a safe space where they can be themselves without fear of judgment. While their love may not be accompanied by fireworks and fanfare, it's enduring and enduring, like a timeless love story that withstands the test of time. In the end, it's not the intensity of the desire that matters, but the depth of the connection that defines the strength of their relationship.

Some of the happiest couples I've ever met were low-key, showing very little affection. Not a thing wrong with low desire...it just helps if it is mutual.

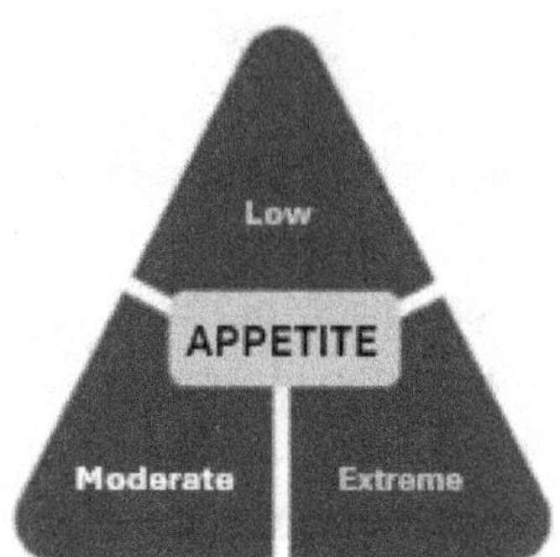
Low
APPETITE
Moderate
Extreme

Moderate

In a relationship where both partners share a moderate level of romantic desire, it's like embarking on a beautiful journey hand in hand, where every moment is infused with warmth and affection. Their love is like a gentle breeze that whispers sweet nothings, igniting sparks of joy and contentment. While their passion may not reach soaring heights, it's the steady, consistent presence of love that keeps their bond strong and flourishing.

In such dynamics, partners find delight in expressing their love through thoughtful gestures and heartfelt words. From surprise date nights to handwritten love notes, they take pleasure in creating special moments that deepen their connection. Their relationship is like a canvas, and they paint it with the colors of affection and tenderness, weaving a tapestry of memories that they'll cherish for a lifetime.

Despite the moderate level of desire, these relationships are characterized by a beautiful balance of intimacy and independence. Partners respect each other's space and autonomy, allowing room for personal growth and exploration. While they enjoy being together, they also nurture their individual passions and interests, enriching their lives both as a couple and as individuals. In the end, it's the harmonious blend of love, respect, and mutual support that makes their relationship truly special.

The couples in this category I've noticed over the years are real busy in their professional lives. The secret to their success is they don't stay around each other very much. But when they get together again, it's like a honeymoon all over again! Whatever works, right?

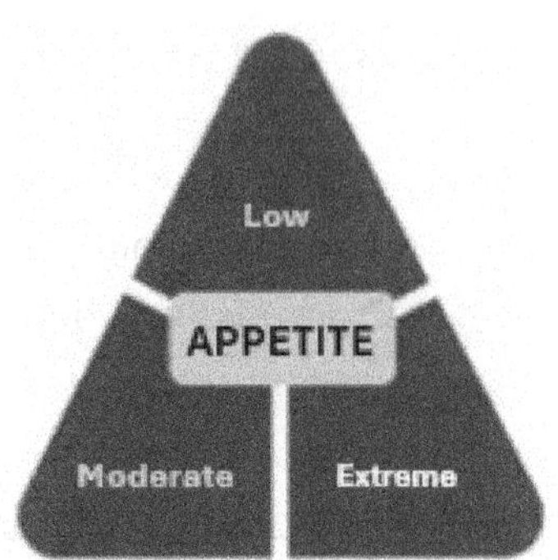

Low
APPETITE
Moderate
Extreme

Extreme

When both partners share an extreme level of romantic desire, it's like fireworks lighting up the sky on a starry night – electrifying, exhilarating, and utterly enchanting. Their love knows no bounds, and every moment spent together feels like a magical adventure. From passionate embraces to whispered declarations of love, their connection is fueled by an intense flame that burns bright and unwavering.

In such dynamics, partners revel in the intensity of their emotions, embracing every opportunity to express their love in bold and extravagant ways. Their relationship is like a whirlwind romance, filled with grand gestures and sweeping declarations of affection. Whether it's planning elaborate surprises or showering each other with lavish gifts, they spare no effort in making each other feel cherished and adored.

Despite the intense level of desire, these relationships are characterized by a deep sense of emotional intimacy and connection. Partners share their hopes, dreams, and fears with each other, trusting in the strength of their bond to weather any storm. Their love is like a fortress, providing a safe haven where they can be their truest selves without fear of judgment or rejection. In the end, it's the depth of their connection and the passion that ignites their souls that makes their relationship a true force to be reckoned with.

While this may sound appealing to some, be aware that this level of desire can lead to sex addiction. The other dynamic with this scenario is that couples who "love hard" oftentimes "fight hard" too. They are both high-strung people and relish in the "make-up sex" that comes after a blow-up argument. It's exhausting and exhilarating at the same time!

Verbal
COMMUNI-
CATION
Written
Action

COMMUNICATION

Communication in a romantic relationship is the cornerstone of a strong and healthy connection. It's like the glue that holds everything together, allowing partners to express their thoughts, feelings, and needs openly and honestly. Without effective communication, misunderstandings can easily arise, leading to resentment, frustration, and distance between partners. By fostering open lines of communication, couples can navigate through challenges, celebrate successes, and deepen their bond with one another.

One of the most crucial aspects of communication in a romantic relationship is the ability to listen actively. It's not just about hearing the words that are spoken but truly understanding the emotions and intentions behind them. When partners listen to each other with empathy and compassion, they create a space where both voices are heard and valued. This lays the foundation for trust and mutual respect, fostering a deeper sense of intimacy and connection.

Moreover, communication in a romantic relationship helps partners to grow and evolve together. By sharing their thoughts, desires, and goals with each other, couples can support one another in pursuing their dreams and aspirations. Whether it's discussing future plans, addressing concerns, or simply checking in with each other regularly, effective communication allows partners to stay aligned and connected on a deeper level. Ultimately, it's through open and honest communication that couples can build a strong foundation for a lasting and fulfilling relationship.

Here's a secret – to get your partner to open up and speak their mind, start with one or two glasses of wine. Works every time!

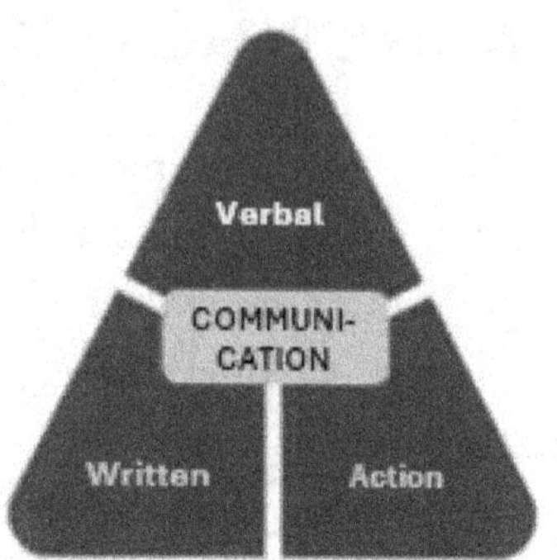
Verbal
COMMUNI-
CATION
Written
Action

Verbal

In a romantic relationship, verbal expression serves as the ultimate superpower, capable of weaving threads of understanding and strengthening the bond between partners. It's like having a magic wand that transforms thoughts and emotions into words, bridging the gap between hearts and minds. When partners verbally express themselves in a clear and heartfelt manner, they create a safe and nurturing environment where honesty and authenticity can thrive.

Verbal expression allows partners to articulate their feelings and needs, fostering deeper emotional intimacy and connection. It's like opening the floodgates of the heart, allowing a torrent of emotions to flow freely between partners. Whether it's saying "I love you" or sharing vulnerable thoughts and insecurities, verbal expression creates a space where partners can be their truest selves without fear of judgment or rejection. This vulnerability strengthens the bond between partners, laying the foundation for trust, empathy, and mutual support.

Moreover, verbal expression serves as a powerful tool for resolving conflicts and addressing misunderstandings in a relationship. It's like shining a light on the dark corners of misunderstanding, illuminating paths to resolution and reconciliation. When partners communicate openly and honestly about their concerns and grievances, they can work together to find mutually beneficial solutions. By actively listening to each other's perspectives and expressing themselves in a respectful and constructive manner, partners can navigate through challenges with grace and understanding, emerging stronger and more united than ever before.

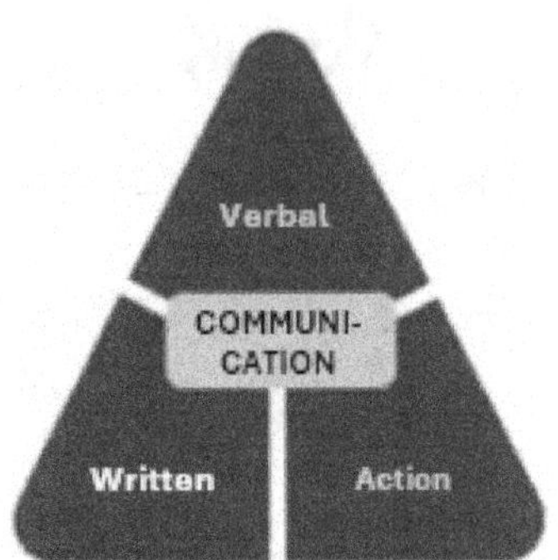
Verbal
COMMUNI-
CATION
Written
Action

Written

Imagine a love note or a heartfelt card as a tiny treasure chest filled with words that sparkle like jewels, waiting to be discovered by your beloved. In a world where digital communication often reigns supreme, there's something undeniably special about putting pen to paper and crafting a message that speaks straight from the heart. Whether it's a simple "I love you" or a detailed expression of admiration, writing love notes and cards allows you to convey your deepest feelings in a tangible and enduring way.

These handwritten tokens of affection serve as timeless reminders of your love and devotion, like little love letters that withstand the test of time. Unlike fleeting text messages or emails that can easily get lost in the digital abyss, love notes and cards have a tangible presence that can be cherished and revisited whenever the heart desires. Whether tucked away in a drawer or proudly displayed on a mantelpiece, these tangible expressions of love serve as constant reminders of the special bond shared between partners.

Moreover, writing love notes and cards provides an opportunity for creativity and self-expression, allowing you to infuse your message with your unique personality and style. Whether you're a poet at heart or someone who struggles to find the right words, there's no wrong way to express your love through writing. From doodling cute illustrations to penning heartfelt verses, each love note and card becomes a reflection of your love story, capturing the essence of your relationship in a way that only you can. So, the next time you want to show your partner just how much they mean to you, why not pick up a pen and let your heart do the talking?

Yeah, you can text but the old-fashioned way of giving letters and cards still pulls the heart strings.

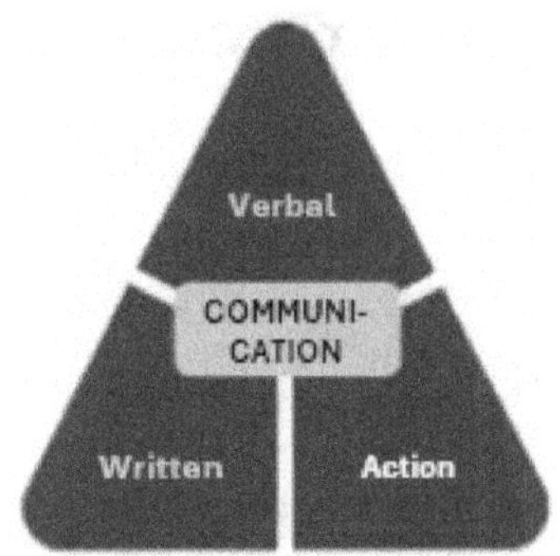
Verbal
COMMUNI-
CATION
Written
Action

Action

"Don't just say you love me...show me!" Sound familiar?

Showing someone that you love them is like painting a masterpiece with the colors of affection, each brushstroke a unique expression of your adoration. From grand gestures to simple acts of kindness, there are countless ways to let your loved one know just how much they mean to you. It's not just about saying "I love you" but demonstrating your love through meaningful actions that speak volumes.

One of the most powerful ways to show someone that you love them is through acts of service. Whether it's cooking their favorite meal, doing household chores, or running errands on their behalf, these acts of selflessness demonstrate your commitment to their happiness and well-being. By taking the time to anticipate their needs and alleviate their burdens, you show your loved one that you're willing to go above and beyond to make their life easier and more enjoyable.

Another way to express your love is through quality time spent together. In today's fast-paced world, carving out dedicated time to be with your loved one speaks volumes about the importance you place on your relationship. Whether it's going for a leisurely walk, having a cozy movie night at home, or simply enjoying each other's company over a cup of coffee, these moments of togetherness create cherished memories that strengthen your bond and deepen your connection.

Some years ago, I dated a great lady and on one particular occasion (I think it was an anniversary of some kind that we had) she kidnapped me at work to go on a weekend excursion at a B&B. She arranged for my car to be picked up at work and parked in my garage. The whole weekend was dedicated to her spoiling me (and of course I reciprocated). It was spontaneous, a great surprise and I fell in love with her all over again. That was about 25 years ago! I still remember it like it was yesterday.

Weekly
PLANNING
Quarterly
Creative

PLANNING

Planning for times to be romantic is like planting seeds of love that bloom into beautiful moments of connection and intimacy. In the hustle and bustle of everyday life, it's easy for romance to take a backseat amidst deadlines, responsibilities, and distractions. However, setting aside dedicated time to be romantic is essential for nurturing the flame of passion and keeping the spark alive in your relationship.

By planning for romantic moments, you demonstrate to your partner that they are a priority in your life. It's like sending a clear message that says, "You are important to me, and I cherish our relationship." Whether it's scheduling a candlelit dinner, planning a surprise weekend getaway, or organizing a cozy movie night at home, these intentional gestures show your commitment to nurturing your connection and creating lasting memories together.

Moreover, planning for romantic moments allows you to escape the monotony of routine and infuse excitement into your relationship. It's like adding a splash of color to a blank canvas, transforming ordinary moments into extraordinary experiences. Whether you're exploring new places, trying new activities, or simply spending quality time together, these planned moments of romance create opportunities for adventure, spontaneity, and joy. So, the next time you want to show your partner just how much they mean to you, why not take the time to plan for a special romantic moment that will leave a lasting impression on their heart?

Weekly
PLANNING
Quarterly   Creative

Weekly

Setting aside one day a week to be with your romantic partner is like carving out a sacred space in your busy schedule dedicated to nurturing your relationship. It's a beautiful commitment to prioritize each other amidst the hustle and bustle of daily life, ensuring that your bond remains strong and vibrant. Whether it's a cozy Sunday afternoon or a lively Friday evening, this designated day becomes a cherished tradition that you both look forward to with excitement and anticipation.

On this special day, you have the opportunity to reconnect with your partner on a deeper level, away from the distractions and demands of the outside world. It's like pressing pause on the chaos of life and immersing yourselves fully in each other's company. Whether you spend the day exploring new places, indulging in shared hobbies, or simply enjoying each other's presence at home, this uninterrupted time together strengthens your bond and deepens your connection.

Moreover, setting aside one day a week to be with your romantic partner reinforces the importance of quality time in nurturing a healthy relationship. It's like watering a plant, ensuring that it receives the nourishment it needs to grow and flourish. By consistently dedicating time to be together, you create a sense of security and stability in your relationship, fostering trust, intimacy, and mutual support. So, whether you're planning a romantic date night or a relaxed day at home, make the most of this precious time with your partner and savor every moment spent together.

Weekly
PLANNING
Quarterly
Creative

Quarterly

Setting aside one weekend every quarter to be with your romantic partner is like embarking on a mini adventure that rejuvenates your relationship and creates lasting memories. In the hustle and bustle of everyday life, it's easy for weeks and months to fly by without truly connecting with your partner. However, by carving out this dedicated time together, you're making a conscious effort to prioritize your relationship and nurture the bond you share.

This quarterly tradition becomes a much-anticipated escape from the routine of daily life, offering an opportunity to unwind, recharge, and reconnect with your partner. Whether you choose to explore a new destination, indulge in a relaxing staycation, or simply enjoy each other's company at home, this uninterrupted time together allows you to deepen your connection and create cherished moments that strengthen your bond.

Moreover, setting aside one weekend a quarter to be with your romantic partner provides a valuable opportunity to break away from the monotony of the everyday and inject excitement into your relationship. It's like adding a splash of spontaneity to your lives, infusing your time together with adventure and joy. Whether you're trying new experiences, revisiting old favorites, or simply embracing the freedom to be fully present with each other, this dedicated time becomes a cherished tradition that you both eagerly anticipate. So, the next time you're planning your calendar, why not mark off one weekend every quarter to devote to your relationship? It's an investment in your love story that pays dividends in happiness and fulfillment.

Weekly
PLANNING
Quarterly
Creative

Creative

Calling all lovebirds! Get ready to sprinkle some extra romance into your relationship with these creative ideas for couples to explore together. Whether you're planning a special date night or looking for ways to add some excitement to your routine, these fun and imaginative activities are sure to ignite sparks of passion and create unforgettable memories.

Picnic under the Stars: Pack a cozy blanket, some delicious snacks, and a bottle of your favorite wine, then head to a scenic spot where you can stargaze together. Whether it's a secluded beach, a lush park, or even your own backyard, spending an evening under the stars is the perfect way to enjoy each other's company in a romantic setting. Bring along a telescope or simply lie back and enjoy the beauty of the night sky as you cuddle up with your partner.

Cooking Class for Two: Put on your chef hats and aprons and enroll in a cooking class together. Whether you're learning how to make mouthwatering Italian pasta, mastering the art of sushi rolling, or whipping up decadent desserts, cooking together is a fun and interactive way to bond as a couple. Plus, you'll get to enjoy the delicious fruits of your labor together, making for a memorable date night that satisfies both your hearts and your taste buds.

Scavenger Hunt Adventure: Plan a scavenger hunt around your city or town, complete with clues that lead you to hidden gems and romantic spots. Get creative with your clues, incorporating inside jokes, shared memories, and special places that hold significance for both of you. Whether you're exploring local landmarks, hunting for treasures in antique shops, or indulging in sweet treats at your favorite bakery, a scavenger hunt adventure is a thrilling way to discover new places and create lasting memories together. So, grab your partner's hand, let your imagination run wild, and embark on an unforgettable romantic journey together!

(Bonus Chapter) Budget-Friendly

Who says romance has to break the bank? Here are some budget-friendly ideas for romantic couples to enjoy together without breaking your budget:

DIY Spa Night: Transform your home into a relaxing spa retreat with DIY facials, massages, and aromatherapy. Create a cozy ambiance with scented candles, soothing music, and fluffy robes, then take turns pampering each other with homemade treatments. From face masks made with kitchen ingredients to foot massages with scented oils, a spa night at home is the perfect way to unwind and reconnect without spending a fortune.

Outdoor Movie Night: Set up a cozy outdoor movie theater in your backyard or balcony with blankets, pillows, and a portable projector. Choose a romantic movie or your favorite classics, then snuggle up under the stars as you enjoy a movie night under the open sky. Pop some popcorn, pour some homemade lemonade or hot cocoa, and let the magic of cinema transport you to a world of romance and adventure.

Picnic in the Park: Pack a picnic basket with homemade sandwiches, fresh fruits, and sweet treats, then head to a nearby park for a romantic picnic al fresco. Spread out a blanket under a shady tree, soak up the sunshine, and enjoy a leisurely meal together surrounded by nature. Take a stroll hand in hand, feed the ducks, or simply bask in each other's company as you savor the simple pleasures of togetherness.

DIY Paint and Sip Night: Channel your inner artists with a DIY paint and sip night at home. Set up a makeshift studio with canvases, paints, brushes, and your favorite beverages, then unleash your creativity as you paint your own masterpieces. Whether you follow along with a step-by-step tutorial or let your imagination run wild, painting together is a fun and romantic way to bond as a couple and create lasting memories.

Remember, it's the thought and effort you put into your time together that truly matters, not the size of your wallet. So, get creative, have fun, and enjoy each other's company as you embark on budget-friendly romantic adventures together!

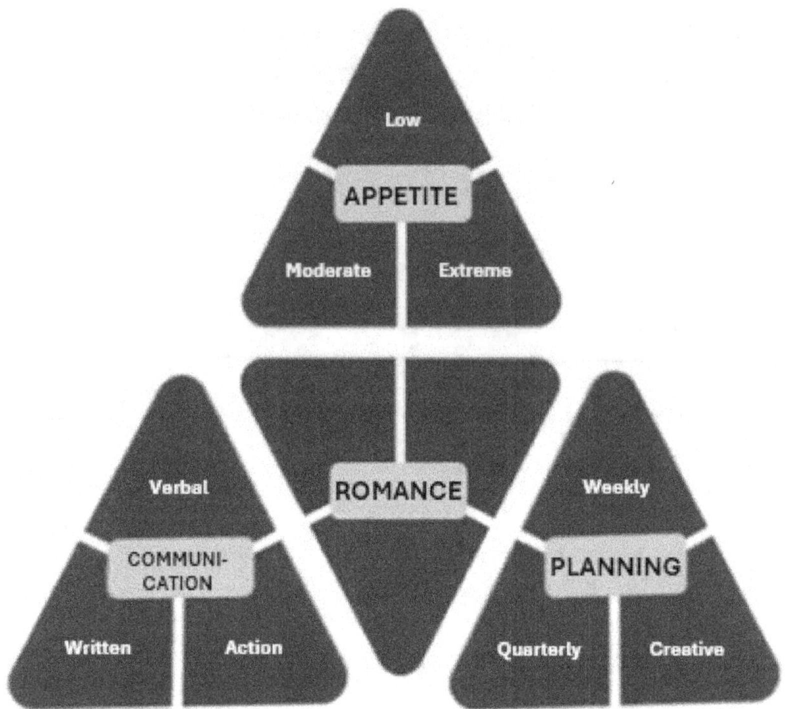
Low
APPETITE
Moderate
Extreme
Verbal
ROMANCE
Weekly
COMMUNI-
CATION
PLANNING
Written
Action
Quarterly
Creative

SUMMARY

Romantic rituals have been woven into the fabric of human relationships for centuries, serving as timeless expressions of love, devotion, and commitment. From exchanging tokens of affection to performing symbolic gestures, these rituals transcend cultures and generations, embodying the universal language of romance that speaks to the depths of the human heart. Whether it's a tender embrace, a passionate kiss, or a heartfelt declaration of love, these rituals form the foundation of our most cherished love stories, passed down through the ages like precious heirlooms.

Throughout history, romantic rituals have played a central role in courtship and courtly love, providing a framework for expressing desire and devotion between partners. From the chivalrous acts of medieval knights to the elaborate courtship rituals of Victorian society, these customs and traditions have shaped our understanding of romance and imbued our relationships with meaning and significance. Whether it's the exchange of love letters, the giving of flowers, or the wearing of wedding rings, these rituals serve as tangible symbols of love that endure through the ages.

Moreover, romantic rituals serve as anchors in the ebb and flow of life, providing comfort and stability amidst the uncertainties of the world. Whether it's a nightly kiss before bedtime, a weekly date night, or an annual anniversary celebration, these rituals create a sense of continuity and security in our relationships, reminding us of the enduring bond we share with our partners. In a world that is constantly changing, these rituals serve as touchstones of love that ground us in the present moment and reaffirm the strength of our connection to one another.

Invitation

Navigating the landscape of relationships can sometimes feel like sailing through stormy seas, with the divorce rate serving as a sobering reminder of the challenges that many couples face. While the idea of "happily ever after" is a cherished dream for many, the reality is that maintaining a long-lasting and fulfilling relationship requires dedication, effort, and resilience. In today's fast-paced world, where the pressures of work, family, and social obligations can take a toll on even the strongest of bonds, couples must confront these challenges head-on and work together to weather the storms of life.

Despite the sobering statistics, it's important to remember that the chances of a relationship lasting forever are not solely determined by external factors such as the divorce rate. While external pressures and societal norms certainly play a role in shaping our perceptions of relationships, the true measure of a couple's longevity lies in their commitment to each other and their willingness to navigate through challenges together. By fostering open communication, practicing empathy and understanding, and prioritizing each other's needs and happiness, couples can build a solid foundation for a lasting and fulfilling relationship.

Moreover, it's essential to recognize that the concept of a relationship lasting forever doesn't necessarily mean that it will be free from conflict or hardship. Every relationship has its ups and downs, its trials and tribulations. What sets successful couples apart is their ability to work through challenges together, to grow and evolve as individuals and as partners, and to emerge stronger and more resilient than ever before. In the end, it's not about avoiding difficulties, but about facing them together with love, patience, and a shared commitment to building a future filled with love and happiness.

In a nutshell, jump in with both feet and give your heart completely to your significant other. The ride might not last forever but while its ongoing, it can create great memories that last a lifetime.

When you're with someone who is sharing their struggles with you...just smile at him/her and give them one of these. He/she will ask "What is that?" Then simply reply "Life Works in Threes."

Other titles coming out:

- Weight Struggles?
- Abundance Struggles?
- Parenting Struggles?
- Life Struggles?
- Purpose Struggles?
- Happiness Struggles?
- Sales Struggles?
- Speaker Struggles?
- Time Struggles?
- Network Struggles?
- Marriage Struggles?
- Divorce Struggles?
- Money Struggles?
- Career Struggles?
- Dating Struggles?
- Caretaker Struggles?
- Forgiveness Struggles?
- Grieving Struggles?
- Success Struggles?
- Golf Struggles?
- Workplace Struggles?
- Stress Struggles?
- Shame/Guilt Struggles?
- Addiction Struggles?

Quotes about Romance

"Romance is thinking about your significant other when you are supposed to be thinking about something else." - Nicholas Sparks

"Romance is the icing, but love is the cake." - Anonymous

"A simple 'I love you' means more than money." - Frank Sinatra

"Love is like the wind, you can't see it, but you can feel it." - Nicholas Sparks

"Love is friendship that has caught fire." - Ann Landers

Here are some common things that **men** often look for in a
romantic relationship:

1. **Physical attraction**: This is usually the initial spark
    that draws men to someone.
2. **Emotional connection**: Men seek someone with
    whom they can connect on a deeper emotional level,
    sharing thoughts, feelings, and experiences.
3. **Mutual respect**: Respect is fundamental in any
    relationship, and men appreciate partners who value
    and respect them for who they are.
4. **Trust**: Trustworthiness and reliability are crucial for
    building a strong foundation in a relationship.
5. **Support**: Men appreciate partners who are supportive
    during both good times and challenging moments.
6. **Shared interests**: Having common hobbies or
    interests can strengthen the bond between partners
    and provide opportunities for shared experiences.
7. **Communication**: Effective communication is key for
    resolving conflicts, expressing needs, and
    understanding each other.
8. **Intimacy**: This includes both physical intimacy
    (affection, sex) and emotional intimacy (closeness,
    vulnerability).
9. **Independence**: While men value connection, they
    also appreciate partners who have their own interests,
    goals, and independence.
10. **Sense of humor**: A compatible sense of humor can
    make interactions enjoyable and lighten the mood
    during tough times.
11. **Compatibility**: Men often look for partners who
    share similar values, goals, and life aspirations.

12. **Growth and encouragement**: They appreciate partners who encourage personal growth and development, both individually and as a couple.
13. **Commitment**: Men typically seek relationships that are committed and monogamous, where both partners are invested in building a future together.

These preferences can vary widely among individuals, but these are some common themes that men often prioritize in their romantic relationships.

Here are some common things that **women** often look for in a romantic relationship:

1. **Respect**: Women seek partners who respect them as individuals, their opinions, and their boundaries.
2. **Trustworthiness**: Trust is essential for women in a relationship, knowing they can rely on their partner and feel secure.
3. **Emotional connection**: Women value deep emotional bonds and want to feel understood and supported by their partner.
4. **Communication**: Effective communication is crucial for resolving conflicts, expressing feelings, and building a strong connection.
5. **Affection and romance**: Many women appreciate gestures of affection, such as thoughtful gestures, compliments, and expressions of love.
6. **Shared values**: Women often look for partners who share similar values, beliefs, and life goals.
7. **Sense of humor**: A compatible sense of humor can create a positive and enjoyable atmosphere in the relationship.
8. **Financial stability**: While not universal, many women appreciate partners who are financially responsible and stable.
9. **Shared interests and activities**: Having common hobbies or interests can strengthen the bond between partners and provide opportunities for shared experiences.
10. **Support**: Women value partners who are supportive of their goals, ambitions, and personal growth.
11. **Integrity**: Women often look for partners who are

honest, dependable, and have strong moral principles.
12. **Commitment**: Women generally seek relationships that are committed and monogamous, where both partners are dedicated to building a future together.
13. **Physical attraction**: While emotional connection is typically more important, physical attraction still plays a role for many women in a romantic relationship.

These preferences can vary greatly from person to person, but these are some common themes that women often prioritize when seeking a romantic partner.

Remember,

When you get right down to it,

Life is about making choices.

Every day, all day long, that's what we do.

- *We choose to get out of bed or not.*
- *We choose to clean up or not.*
- *We choose what to eat all day.*
- *We choose to exercise or not.*
- *We choose to go to work or not.*
- *We choose to do a good job or not.*
- *We choose to come home or not.*
- *We choose to watch TV or do something constructive.*
- *We choose to bed at a decent hour or not.*

And the next day...we start all over again.

What is the meaning of this? Get good at choosing.

Before you can get good at choosing though...you need to understand how life works in threes.

When someone is struggling with a particular area or two, chances are they are "out of balance" with how life works. How does life work? Life works in threes.

If you're interested in personal topics like life, health, money or business topics like sales, time management and public speaking...TRYUNE WORKS! can shed some light on creating success in those areas.

The definition of TRIUNE is a group of three things; united. Being three in one, such as - humans are *mental, physical* and *spiritual beings.* The word TRYUNE is a play of the word TRIUNE, encouraging all to try this concept and help eliminate struggling unnecessarily.

LifeWorksInThrees.com